# Unit 1

**① Read and match.**

Hello, . . .      I'm Bean.

Hello, . . .      I'm Zoko.

Hello, . . .      I'm Poppy.

**② Draw your picture.   Write your name.**

Hello, I'm _____.

2   page two                                                                 Unit 1

③ **Find the names.**

Poppy    Bean    Woody    Zoko

④ **Complete the names.**

1. P _ p p y        3. Z _ k _

2. B _ a _          4. W _ _ d y

Unit 1  page three  3

**⑤ Draw the picture.   Then read and match.**

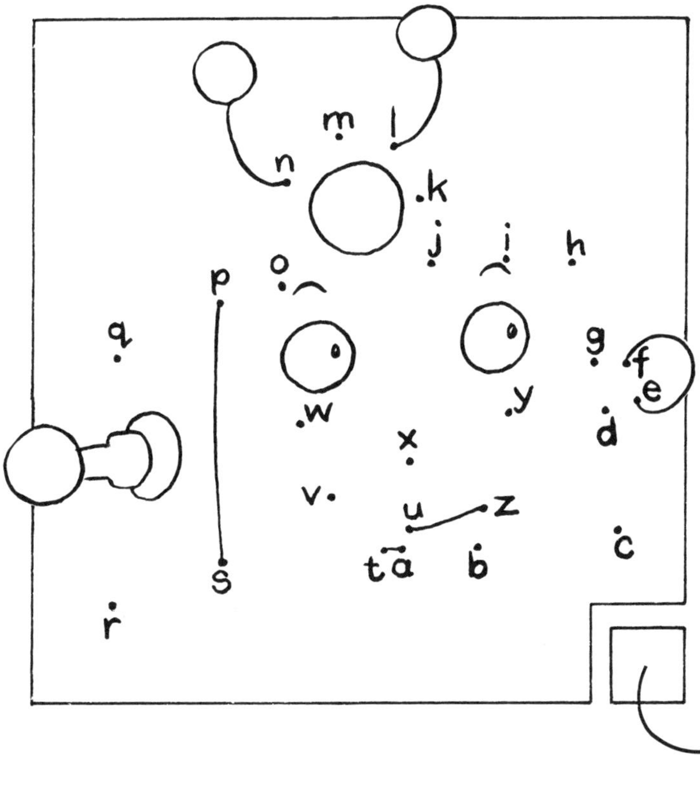

| This is Woody. | This is Poppy. | This is Zoko. | This is Bean. |

**6** **Find the words.**

| hello | what | who | name | yes |
| no | your | my | goodbye | |

# Unit 2

page five 5

**1** **Read and match.**

No.  Goodbye.  Look.  Yes.  Stop.  Listen.

**6** *page six*     Unit 2

## ② Read and match.    Write the letter.

1. a pencil   `C`
2. a cassette   ☐
3. a ruler   ☐
4. a table   ☐

5. a bag   ☐
6. a book   ☐
7. a pen   ☐
8. a rubber   ☐

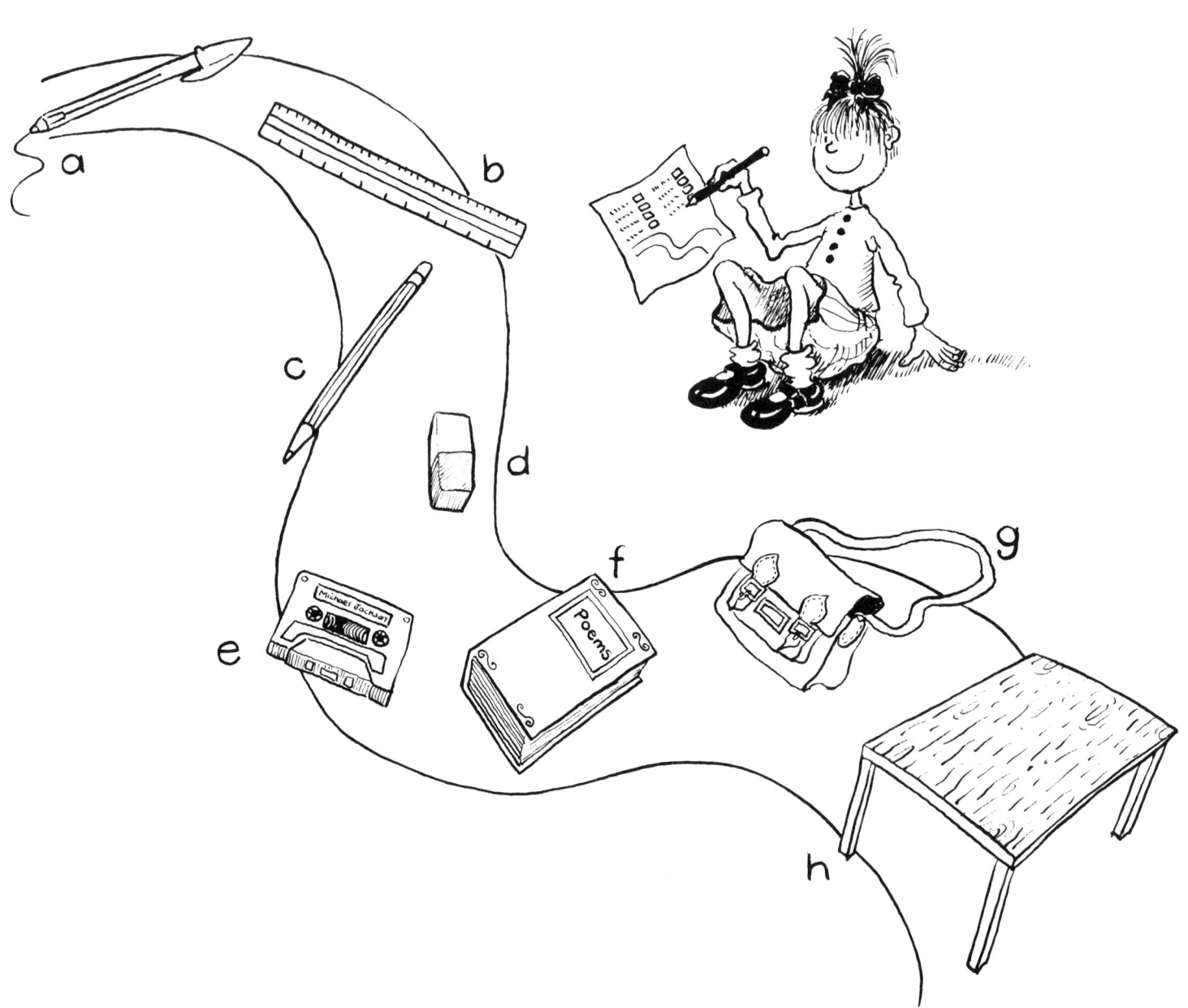

Unit 2     *page seven* **7**

### ③ Complete the sentences.

## 8 page eight  Unit 2

**④ Complete the crossword.**

# Unit 3

page nine  9

① **Read and match.**

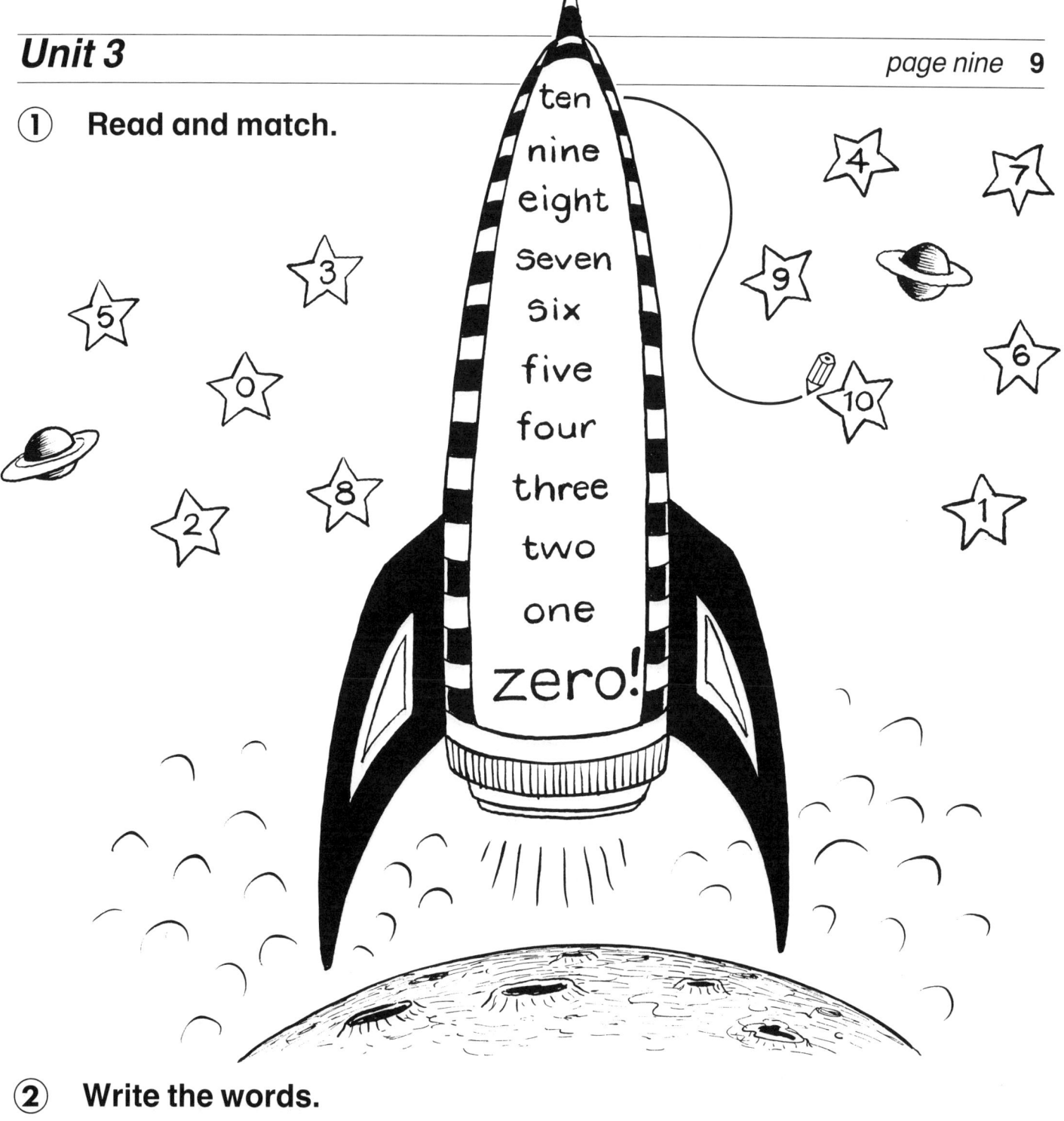

② **Write the words.**

a. one

b. _____

c. _____

d. _____

e. _____

f. _____

③ **Write:** *a* or *an*.

1. <u>an</u> apple
2. ___ book 
3. ___ umbrella
4. ___ bag  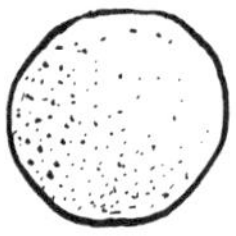 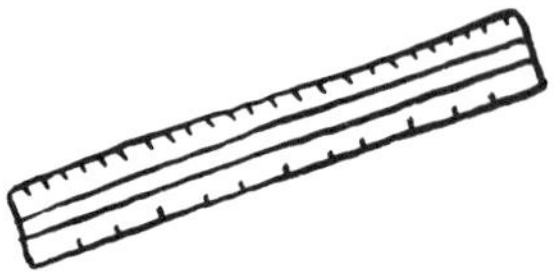
5. ___ cassette
6. ___ ruler
7. ___ orange
8. ___ elephant
9. ___ rubber
10. ___ icecream

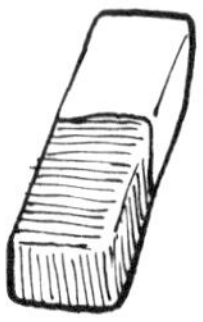

Unit 3  page eleven **11**

④ **Write the words.**

⑤ **Write the answers.**

1. four + five = _nine_
2. three + four = _____
3. two + six = _____
4. one + three = _____

5. seven + three = _____
6. three + two = _____
7. four + two = _____
8. two + one = _____

**6** Complete the sentences.
Choose one word from the box.

# Unit 4

page thirteen  13

**①  Read and match.   Write the letter.**

1. It's an elephant.   b
2. It's a car.
3. It's a doll.
4. It's a football.

5. It's a computer.
6. It's a bicycle.
7. It's a boat.
8. It's an aeroplane.

**14** *page fourteen*          Unit 4

**② Complete the sentences.**

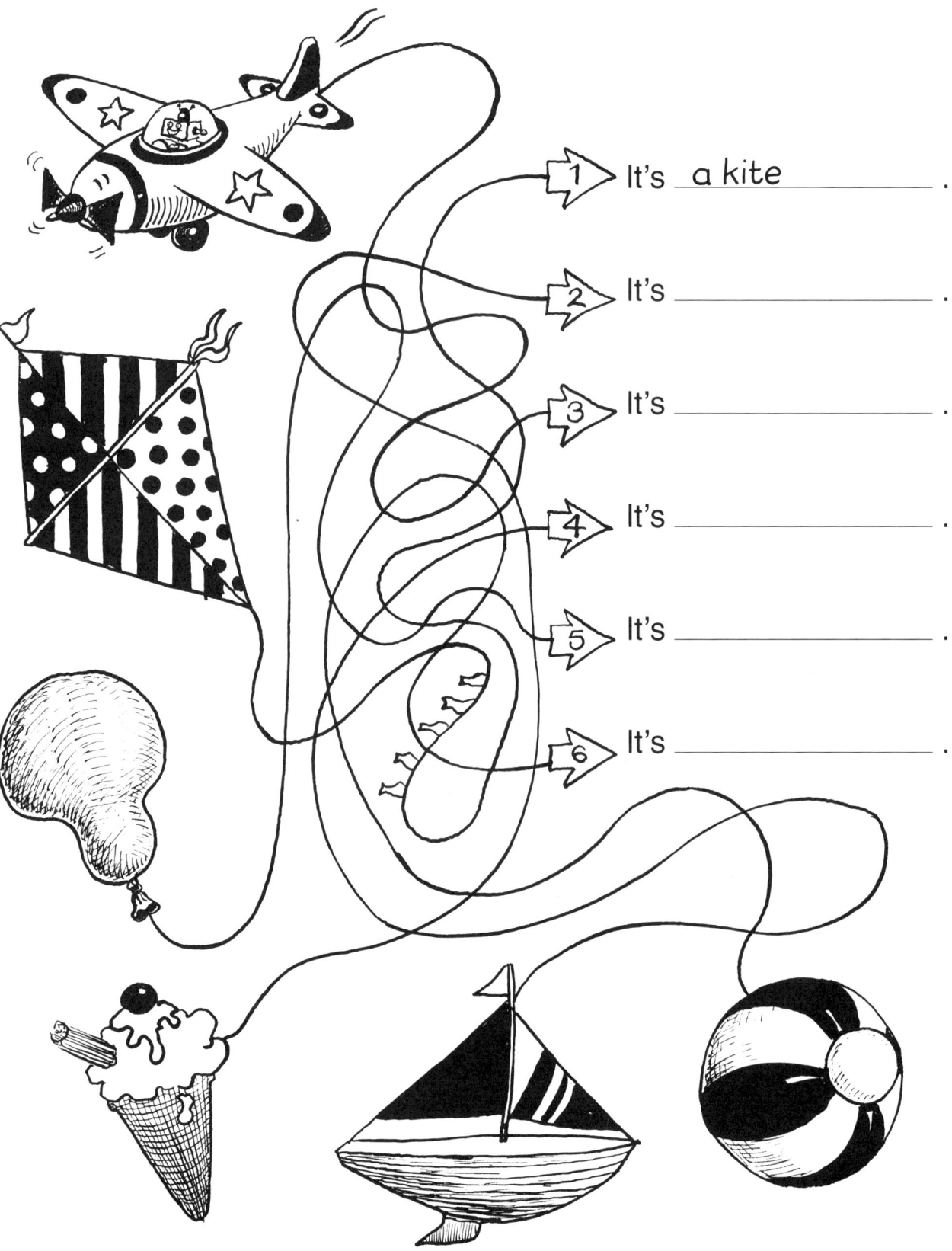

1  It's  a kite            .
2  It's _____ .
3  It's _____ .
4  It's _____ .
5  It's _____ .
6  It's _____ .

③ **Write:** *my* or *your*.

## ④ Find the words. Read and match.

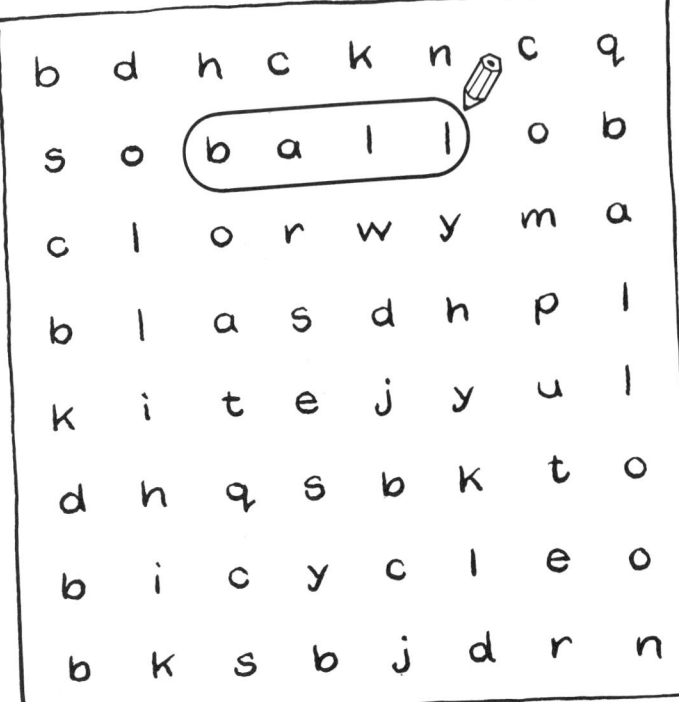

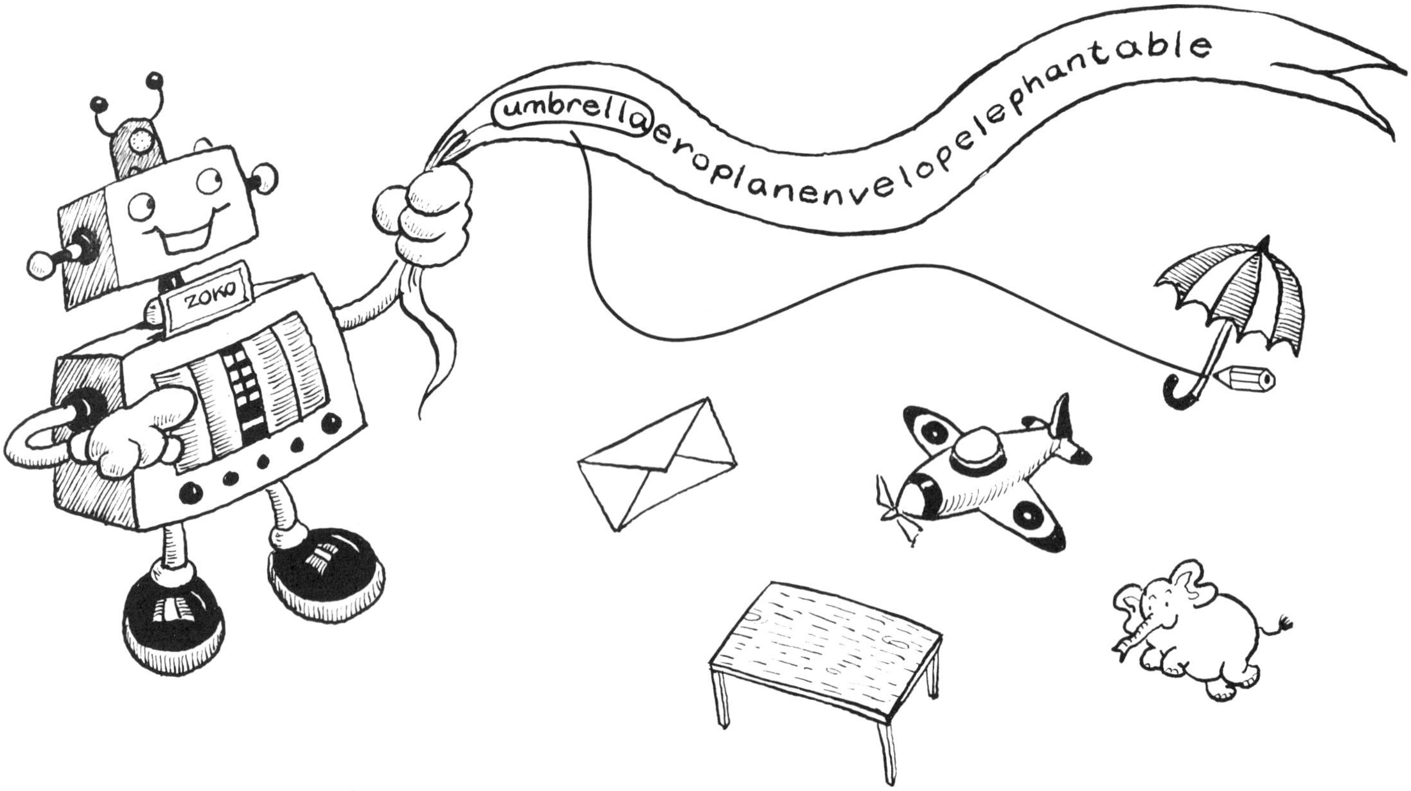
umbrellaeroplanenvelopelephantable
ZOKO

## ⑤ Find the words.

| | | | | | | | |
|---|---|---|---|---|---|---|---|
| b | d | h | c | k | n | c | q |
| s | o | b | a | l | l | o | b |
| c | l | o | r | w | y | m | a |
| b | l | a | s | d | h | p | l |
| k | i | t | e | j | y | u | l |
| d | h | q | s | b | k | t | o |
| b | i | c | y | c | l | e | o |
| b | k | s | b | j | d | r | n |

Ken
boat
ball kite
computer
doll car
balloon
bicycle

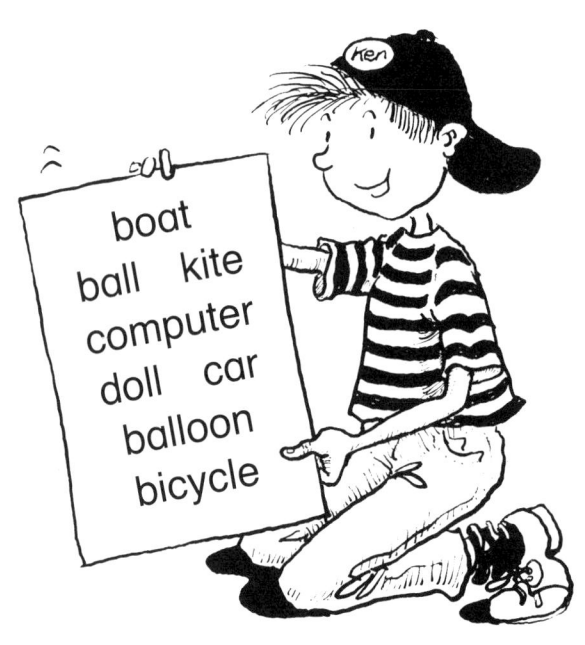

# Unit 5

**①  Write: *he* or *she*.**

1. _____'s seven.
2. _____'s eight.
3. _____'s ten.

4. _____'s ten.
5. _____'s nine.

**②  Write the sentences again.**

1. Poppy is 10.  <u>She's ten.</u>
2. Bean is 10.  _____
3. Woody is 9.  _____
4. Kate is 8.  _____
5. Ken is 10.  _____

6. _____'s five.

Unit 5

③ **Write:** *his* **or** *her*.

1. It's <u>her</u> book.
2. It's ____ bag.
3. It's ____ balloon.
4. It's ____ icecream.
5. It's ____ bicycle.
6. It's ____ ball.
7. It's ____ aeroplane.
8. It's ____ ruler.

Unit 5     page nineteen 19

**④ Complete the sentences. Write: *am ('m)* or *is ('s)*.**

**⑤ Write the sentences.**

1. It's an envelope.

2. _____

3. _____

4. _____

Unit 5

**6 Complete the crossword.**

# Unit 6

**① Write:** *Yes, it is.* **or** *No, it isn't.*

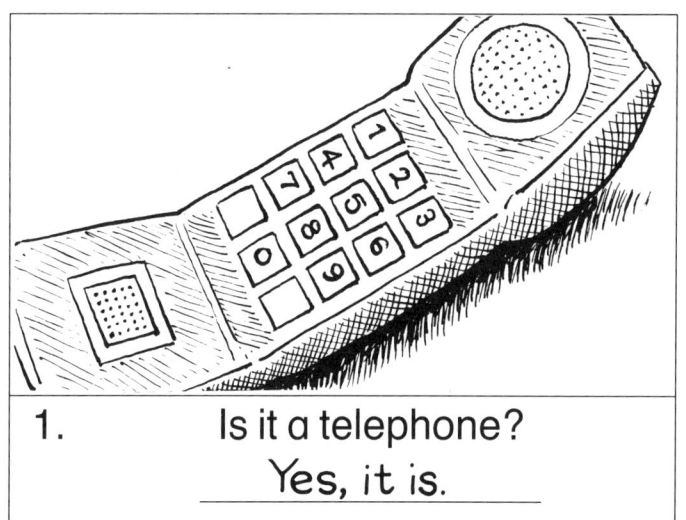

1. Is it a telephone?
   Yes, it is.

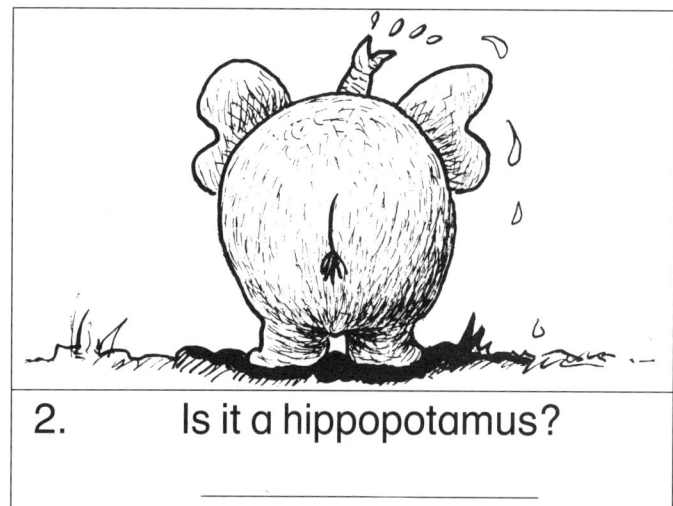

2. Is it a hippopotamus?

3. Is it a calculator?

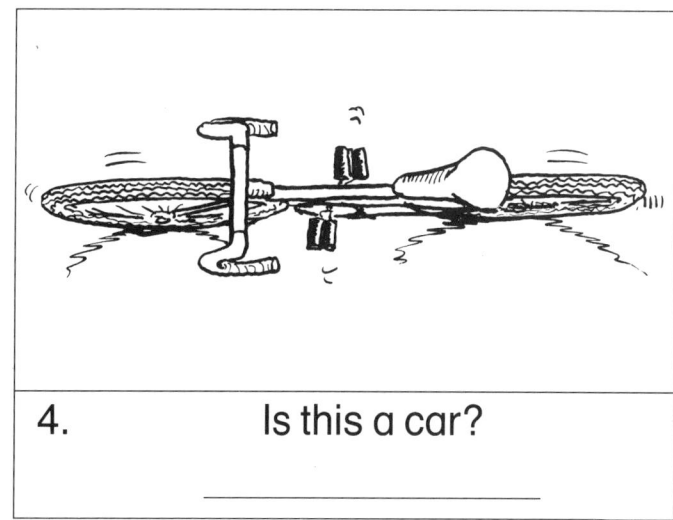

4. Is this a car?

5. Is this a bicycle?

6. Is this a boat?

**22** *page twenty-two*  Unit 6

**2** **Read and match.  Write the letter.**

1. This is the small kite.  `c`
2. This is the big aeroplane. ☐
3. This is the small balloon. ☐
4. This is the small ball. ☐
5. This is the small aeroplane. ☐
6. This is the big kite. ☐
7. This is the big ball. ☐
8. This is the big balloon. ☐

Unit 6  page twenty-three  **23**

③ **Look at the pictures and say the words.**

a   b   c   d

**Match the sounds and the letters.**

a   b   c   d

④ **Complete the words.**

| 1. | 2. | 3. | 4. |
|---|---|---|---|
|  |  |  | 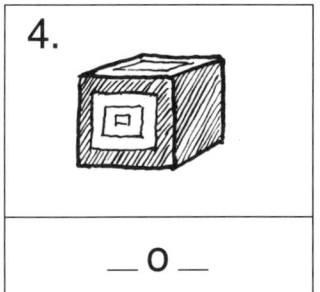 |
| t _ l _ _ h _ n _ | d _ g | d e _ e _ _ i _ e | _ o _ |

24 *page twenty-four*  Unit 6

## ⑤ Write the words.

# Unit 7

**1  Write:** *big* or *small*, *long* or *short*.

Hello! I'm a happy monster.

I've got a __big__ head.

I've got two _____ eyes

and two _____ eyes.

I've got a _____ nose.

I've got _____ hair.

I've got _____ ears

and I've got

a _____ mouth.

**2** **Answer: right (√) or wrong (×)?**

1. My mother has got long hair. ............................. √ ×
2. My father has got a big nose. ............................. √ ×
3. My brother has got big ears. ............................. √ ×
4. My big sister has got short hair. ......................... √ ×
5. My little sister has got big eyes. ......................... √ ×

**3** **Draw your face here.  Complete the sentences.**

Write: *long* or *short*, *big* or *small*.

1. I've got _____ hair.
2. I've got _____ eyes.
3. I've got a _____ mouth.

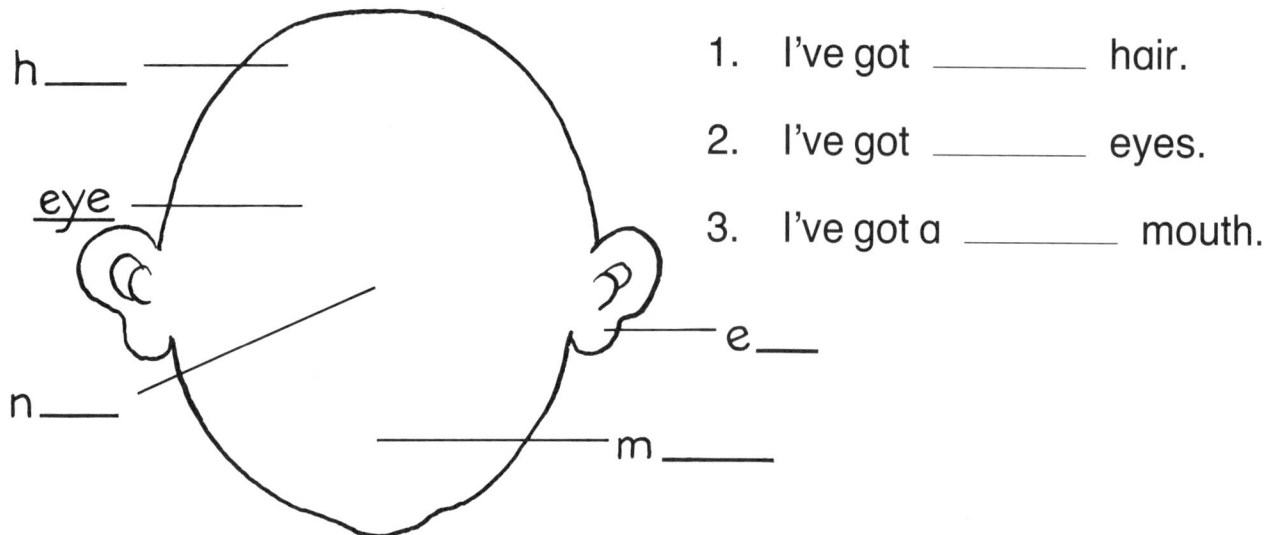

Unit 7                                    page twenty-seven  **27**

④  **Look at the pictures and say the words.**

**Match the sounds and the letters.**

⑤  **Find the family words.**

| letter | detective | (mother) | sister | nose |
| father | ear | hair | long | brother | mouth | eye |

**28** *page twenty-eight*          Unit 7

**6**    **Read and match.**    **Write the letter.**

1. She's got a bag.   `a`      4. She's got an icecream. ☐
2. He's got an icecream. ☐      5. He's got a bag. ☐
3. He's got three pens. ☐      6. She's got three pens. ☐

# Unit 8

**(1) Write: Yes, I have. or No, I haven't.**

1. Have you got a sister? _____
2. Have you got a brother? _____
3. Have you got long hair? _____
4. Have you got big eyes? _____
5. Have you got a bicycle? _____
6. Have you got a computer? _____

**(2) Read and match.**

Daisy is my cousin. She's got long hair. She's got big eyes and a small nose. She's got a big mouth and she's got small ears.

**Now write: Yes, she has. or No, she hasn't.**

1. Has Daisy got big eyes? _____
2. Has Daisy got long hair? _____
3. Has Daisy got a big nose? _____

Unit 8

### 3. Write: *Yes, he has. / No, he hasn't.*
or *Yes, she has. / No, she hasn't.*

1. Has Uncle Paul got an old dog?  No, he hasn't.
2. Has Uncle Paul got a fat dog?  _____
3. Has Auntie Lynn got a happy dog?  _____
4. Has Cousin Pat got a fat dog?  _____
5. Has Cousin Pat got a thin dog?  _____
6. Has Lucy got a tall dog?  _____
7. Has Cousin Daisy got a thin dog?  _____
8. Has Cousin Daisy got an old dog?  _____

Unit 8  page thirty-one  31

④ **Look at the pictures and say the words.**

**Match the sounds and the letters.**

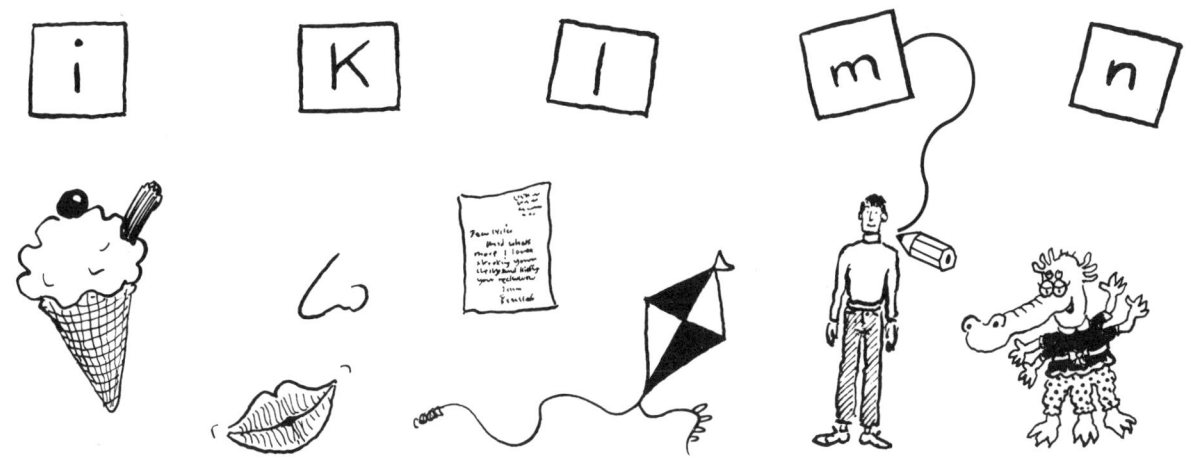

⑤ **Complete the sentences.   Choose one word from the box.**

| sad | thin | short | happy | tall | fat | old |

1. This boy is _tall_ .
2. This girl is _____ .
3. This man is _____ .
4. This woman is _____ .
5. This monster is _____ .
6. This robber is _____ .
7. This detective is _____ .

**6** **Find the words.**

| short | tall | young |
| old | thin | fat |
| sad | happy | lazy |
| small | big | long |

# Unit 9

**1** **Write:** *Yes, I can.* **or** *No, I can't.*

1. Can you see a bird in a cage?  <u>Yes, I can.</u>
2. Can you see an aeroplane?  _____
3. Can you see a photograph?  _____
4. Can you see a computer?  _____
5. Can you see a telephone?  _____
6. Can you see a calculator?  _____
7. Can you see a ball?  _____
8. Can you see an envelope?  _____

## ② Complete the sentences.

1. The lion is ___Annie___'s kite.
2. The hippo is _____'s kite.
3. The snake is _____'s kite.
4. The bird is _____'s kite.
5. The giraffe is _____ ____ .
6. The monkey is _____ ____ .

Shep   Annie   Caroline   Lucy   Ken   Herman

Unit 9  page thirty-five  35

**③ Look at the pictures and say the words.**

**Match the sounds and the letters.**

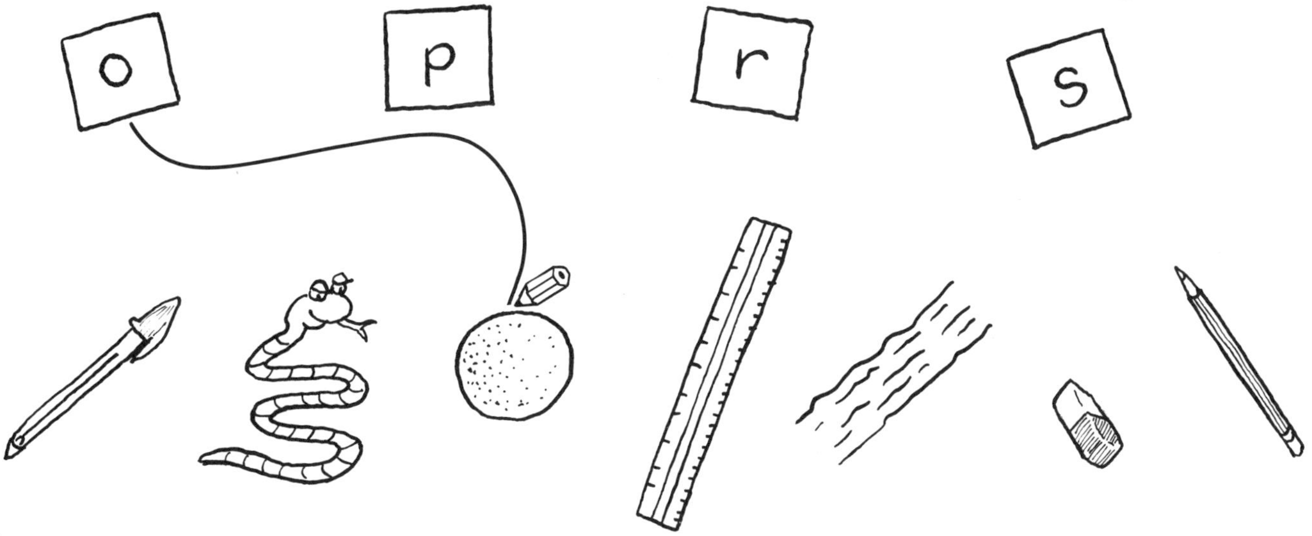

**④ Complete the words.**

1.    _ o _ k e _

3.    _ i _ _

2.    _ n _ _ e

4.    _ _ e _ a _ _

## 5) Read. Match the questions and answers.

1. Is this Lifter's map?
2. Whose photo is this?
3. Can you see Mr X's boat?
4. Whose television is this?

a. No, we can't. It isn't here now.
b. It's Lifter's photo.
c. It's my cousin's TV, I think.
d. No. This is Captain Shadow's map.

## 6) Can you say this?

ZYXWVUTSRQPONMLKJIHGFEDCBA

**Can you read this?**

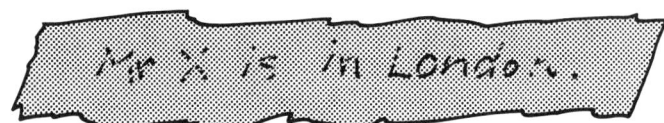
Mr X is in London.

**Can you draw this picture?**

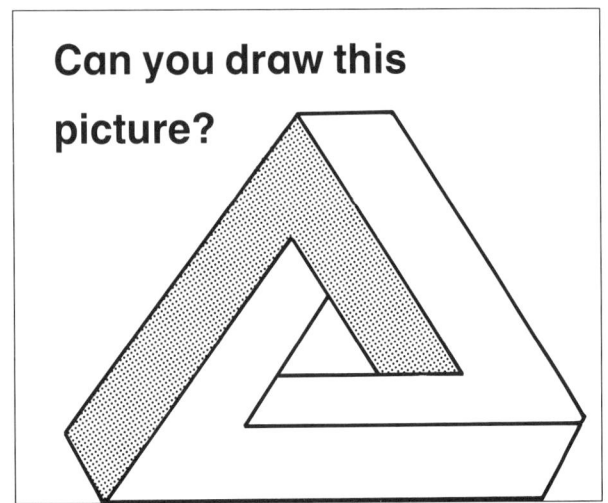

# Unit 10

page thirty-seven  **37**

**① Complete the sentences.   Choose one word from the box.**

| elephant   dog   bird   snake   lion   monkey |
|---|

**Then colour the pictures.**

1.

The _____
has got a red apple.

2.

The _____
has got a blue umbrella.

3.

The _____
has got a blue ball.

4.

The _____
is in a green box.

5.

The _____
is in a yellow cage.

6.

The _____
is on a black bicycle.

**38** *page thirty-eight*  Unit 10

**② Draw and then colour the clothes.**

1. a blue hat

2. a pair of yellow shoes

3. a red skirt

4. a green shirt

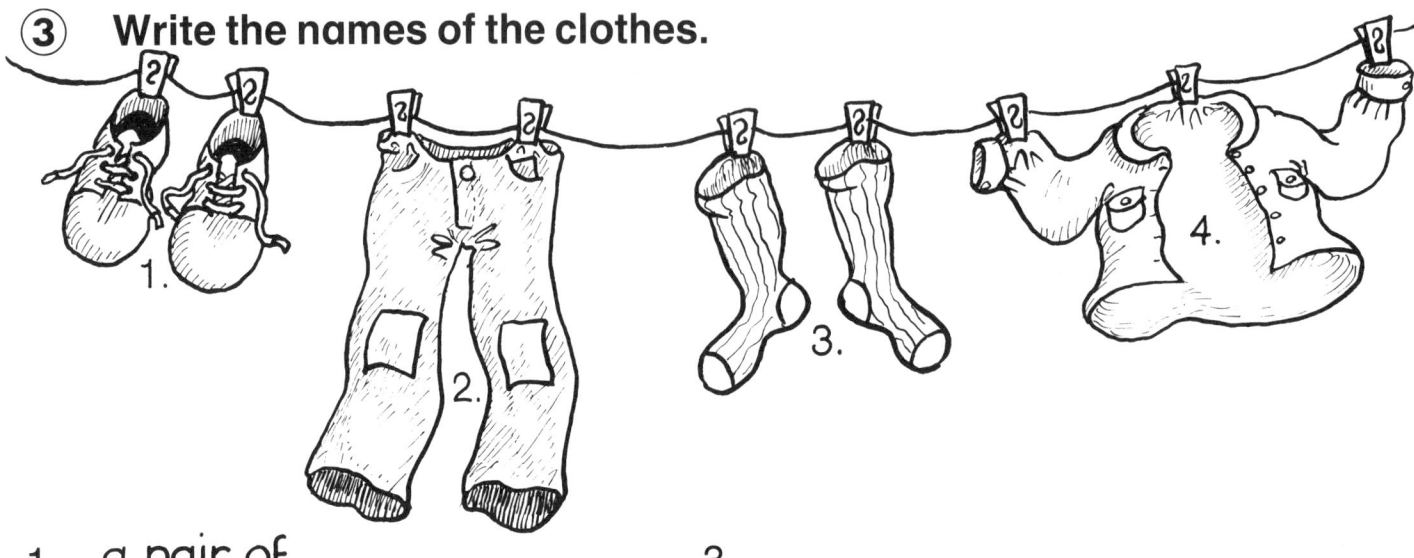

**③ Write the names of the clothes.**

1. a pair of _____

2. _____

3. _____

4. _____

Unit 10  page thirty-nine  39

④  **Look at the pictures and say the words.**

t   u   w   z

**Match the sounds and the letters.**

t   u   w   z

⑤  **Find the clothes words.**

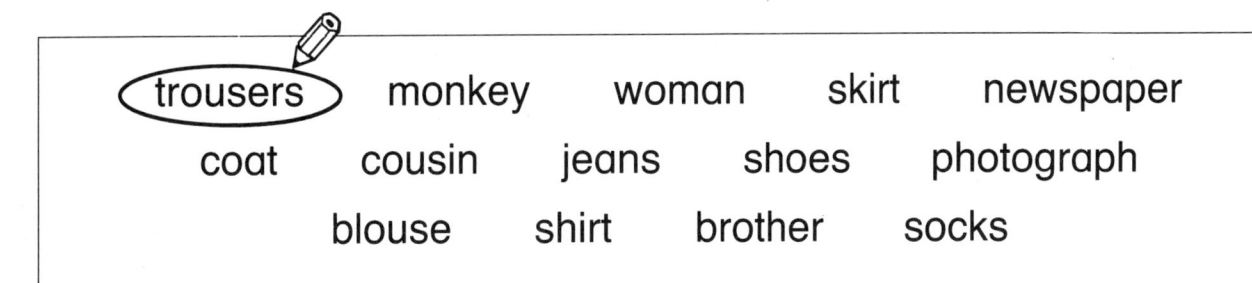

trousers   monkey   woman   skirt   newspaper
coat   cousin   jeans   shoes   photograph
blouse   shirt   brother   socks

40 *page forty*  Unit 10

**6** **Read and match. Write the letter.**

1. The envelope is on the table. ☐
2. The map is on the newspaper. ☐
3. The hat is on the monkey's head. ☐
4. The shoes are in the small bag. ☐
5. The blouse is in the big bag. ☐
6. The calculator is on the desk. ☐

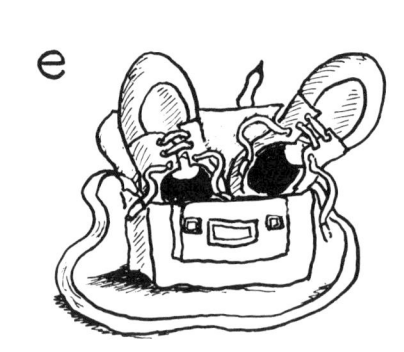

**Now colour the pictures.**

a. The map is blue.
b. The envelope is yellow.
c. The blouse is green.
d. The desk is brown.
e. The small bag is red.
f. The hat is black.

# Unit 11

page forty-one  **41**

① **Answer: right (✓) or wrong (✗)?**

1. This monster is big and fat. ........................................... ✓ ✗
2. He's got four arms. ................................................... ✓ ✗
3. He's got very big hands. ............................................. ✓ ✗
4. He's got three legs. .................................................. ✓ ✗
5. His legs are very long. ............................................... ✓ ✗
6. He's got small knees. ................................................ ✓ ✗
7. He's got four big eyes. .............................................. ✓ ✗
8. He's got one mouth for boys and one mouth for girls. ..... ✓ ✗

42  *page forty-two*  Unit 11

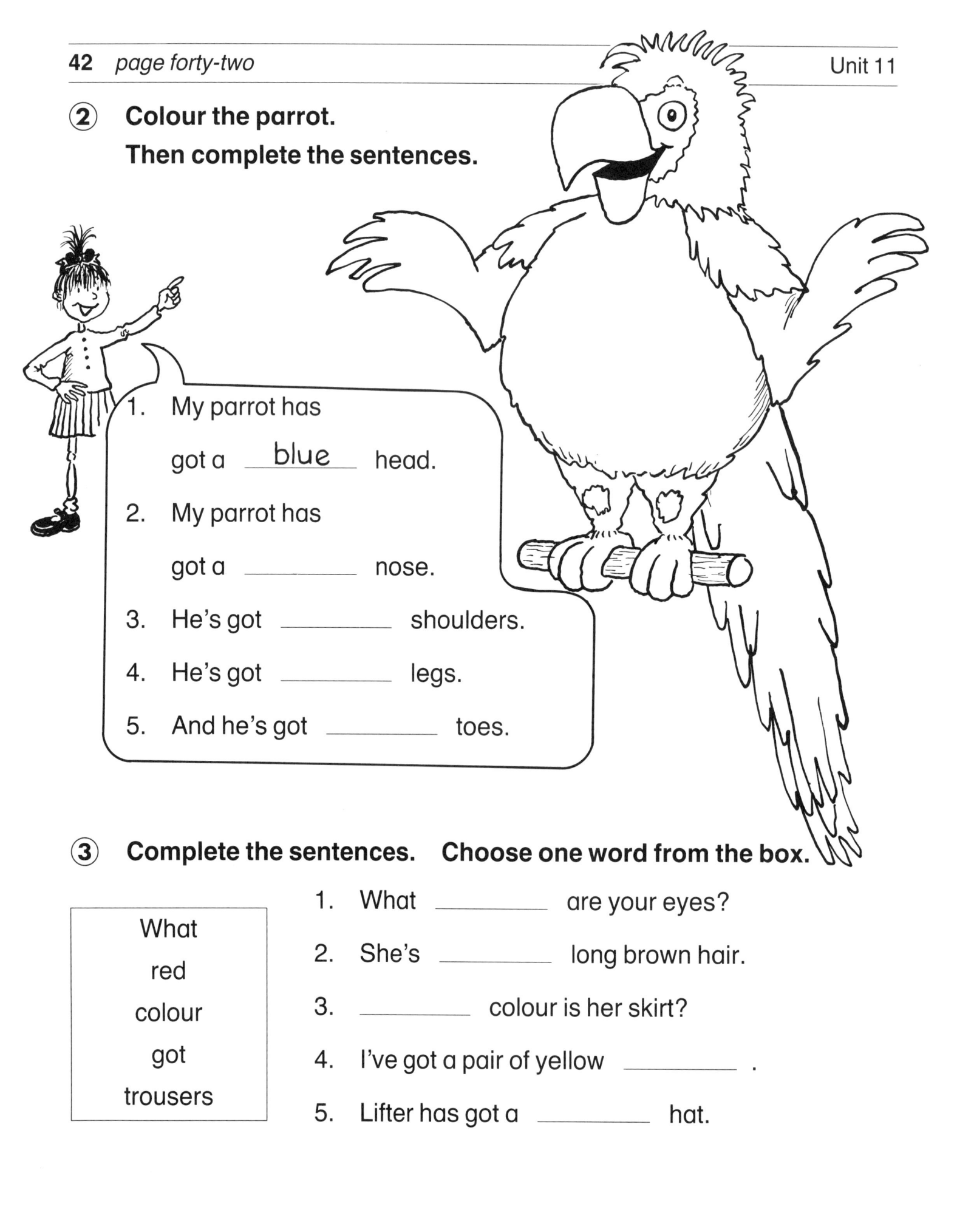

**② Colour the parrot.**
**Then complete the sentences.**

1. My parrot has got a __blue__ head.
2. My parrot has got a _____ nose.
3. He's got _____ shoulders.
4. He's got _____ legs.
5. And he's got _____ toes.

**③ Complete the sentences.  Choose one word from the box.**

| What |
| red |
| colour |
| got |
| trousers |

1. What _____ are your eyes?
2. She's _____ long brown hair.
3. _____ colour is her skirt?
4. I've got a pair of yellow _____ .
5. Lifter has got a _____ hat.

Unit 11 page forty-three 43

## ④ Listen to your teacher.
**Listen to the *a* sound in the words.**

apple       car

**Repeat the words.**

**Now say these words.**

| hand | arm | map | happy | father | man |
| family | party | bank | are | black | plan |

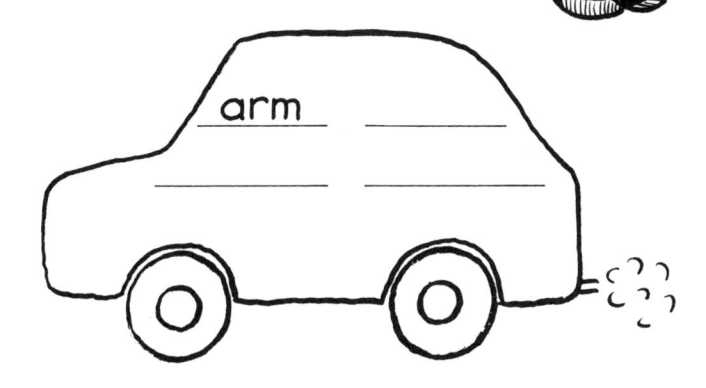

**Write the words with the same *a* sound together.**

hand ___

arm ___

## ⑤ Complete the words.

1. n e _ s _ a _ e _

2. _ e a _

3. t _ o u _ e _ _

4. _ a _ _

Unit 11

## 6 Complete the crossword.

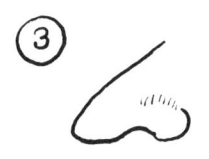

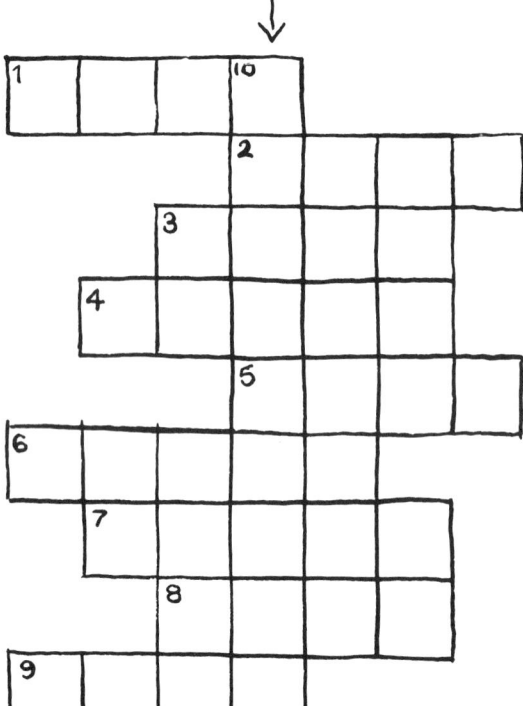

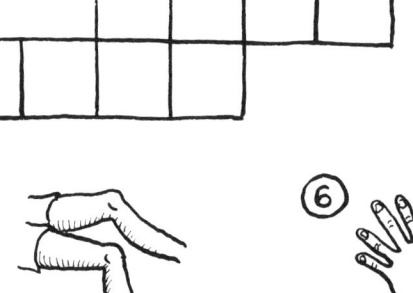

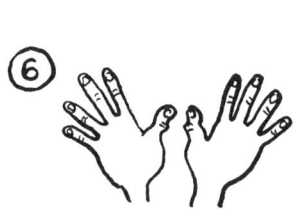

1. (ear)
2. (hair)
3. (nose)
4. (mouth)
5. (knee)
6. (hands)
7. (shoulder)
8. (body)
9. (feet)
10. (eyes)

## 7 Write: *have* or *has*.

1. Kate _____ got black hair.
2. Ken _____ got a hat on his head.
3. Ken and Kate _____ got happy faces.
4. _____ they got big noses?
5. _____ Kate got her parrot on her shoulder?

# Unit 12

*page forty-five* **45**

**① Read and match. Write the letter.**

1. There's a snake in the hat. ☐
2. There's one rabbit in the hat. ☐
3. There are two monkeys in the hat. ☐
4. There's one monkey in the hat. ☐
5. There's a hat on the monkey's head. ☐
6. There are three rabbits in the hat. ☐

**② Write: *is ('s)* or *are*.**

1. There ____ a hat in my uncle's hand.
2. There ____ three rabbits in the hat.
3. There ____ a snake in the hat.
4. There ____ two monkeys in the hat.
5. There ____ a hat on the monkey's head.

## ③ Read.

In my bag there's an old book. There are two old maps in the book. In my bag there's a big blue hat, and there's a blue and yellow coat too. There are four long green snakes in the bag, and there's a happy parrot on my shoulder.

**Now write:**

*Yes, there is.* **or** *Yes, there are.*

1. Is there an old book in his bag? _____
2. Are there two old maps in the book? _____
3. Is there a hat in his bag? _____
4. Is there a coat in his bag? _____
5. Are there four snakes in the bag? _____
6. Is there a parrot on his shoulder? _____

## ④ Write: *Yes, there is.* **or** *No, there isn't.*

1. Is there a book in your bag now? _____
2. Is there a comic on your desk? _____
3. Is there a pen in your hand now? _____
4. Is there a zoo in your city? _____
5. Is there a snake in your socks? _____
6. Is there a parrot on your shoulder? _____

Unit 12  page forty-seven  **47**

**⑤** **Listen to your teacher.**

**Listen to the** *e* **sound in the words.**

**e**lephant    m**e**

**Repeat the words.**

**Now say these words.**

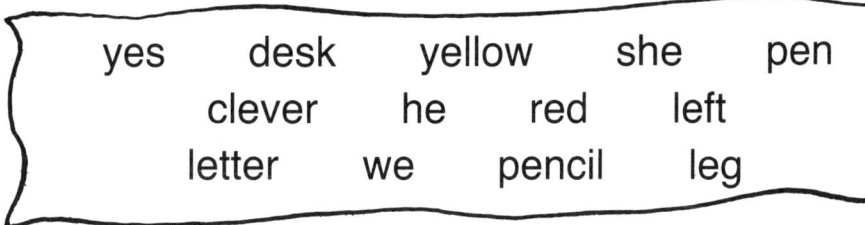

| yes | desk | yellow | she | pen |
|---|---|---|---|---|
| clever | he | red | left | |
| letter | we | pencil | leg | |

**Write the words with the same** *e* **sound together.**

yes

she

**⑥** **Complete the sentences.   Choose one word from the box.**

| Are |
|---|
| There |
| is |
| are |
| there |

1. There _____ six matches in the box now!
2. Is _____ a rabbit in your bag, Uncle?
3. _____ there three birds in the cage now?
4. There _____ a blue hat on my uncle's head.
5. _____ are five snakes in his hat too!

48 page forty-eight  Unit 12

**(7) Find the river.**

**Complete the duck's sentences.**

Remember: ↑ Go straight on.
⌐ Turn right.
¬ Turn left.

Go <u>straight</u> on.

Turn ____ here.

Turn ____ here.

Turn ____ here.

Turn ____ here.

...and turn ____ here.

Turn ____ and go ____.

The River

**(8) Find the animal or bird words.**

| plan | (rabbit) | shoulder | park | monkey | zoo | lion |
| map | head | dog | blouse | duck | cage | parrot |

# Unit 13

*page forty-nine* **49**

**① Write the answers.**

1. How many boys are there in the picture? _____

2. How many girls are there in the picture? _____

3. How many bicycles are there in the picture? _____

4. How many monsters are there in the picture? _____

5. How many cars are there in the picture? _____

50  *page fifty*  Unit 13

**② Write the answers.**

1. How many apples can you see?   I can see five apples.

2. How many newspapers can you see?  _____

3. How many pencils can you see?  _____

4. How many hats can you see?  _____

5. How many boxes of matches can you see?  _____

6. How many envelopes can you see?  _____

7. How many boxes of chocolates can you see?  _____

Unit 13      page fifty-one **51**

**③ Listen to your teacher.**

**Listen to the *i* sound in the words.**

**Repeat the words.**

**Now say these words.**

hippo

ice cream

| I'm | in | fine | comic | hi | kite |
| rabbit | this | bicycle | right | lion | white |
| city | cinema | twins | | | |

**Write the words with the same *i* sound together.**

in ____

____

____

I'm ____

____

____

**④ Write the answers.**

1. How many ears have you got? ____
2. How many toes have you got? ____
3. How many coats have you got? ____
4. How many pairs of shoes have you got? ____
5. How many pens have you got in your bag? ____
6. How many books have you got on your desk? ____

## 5 Find the words.

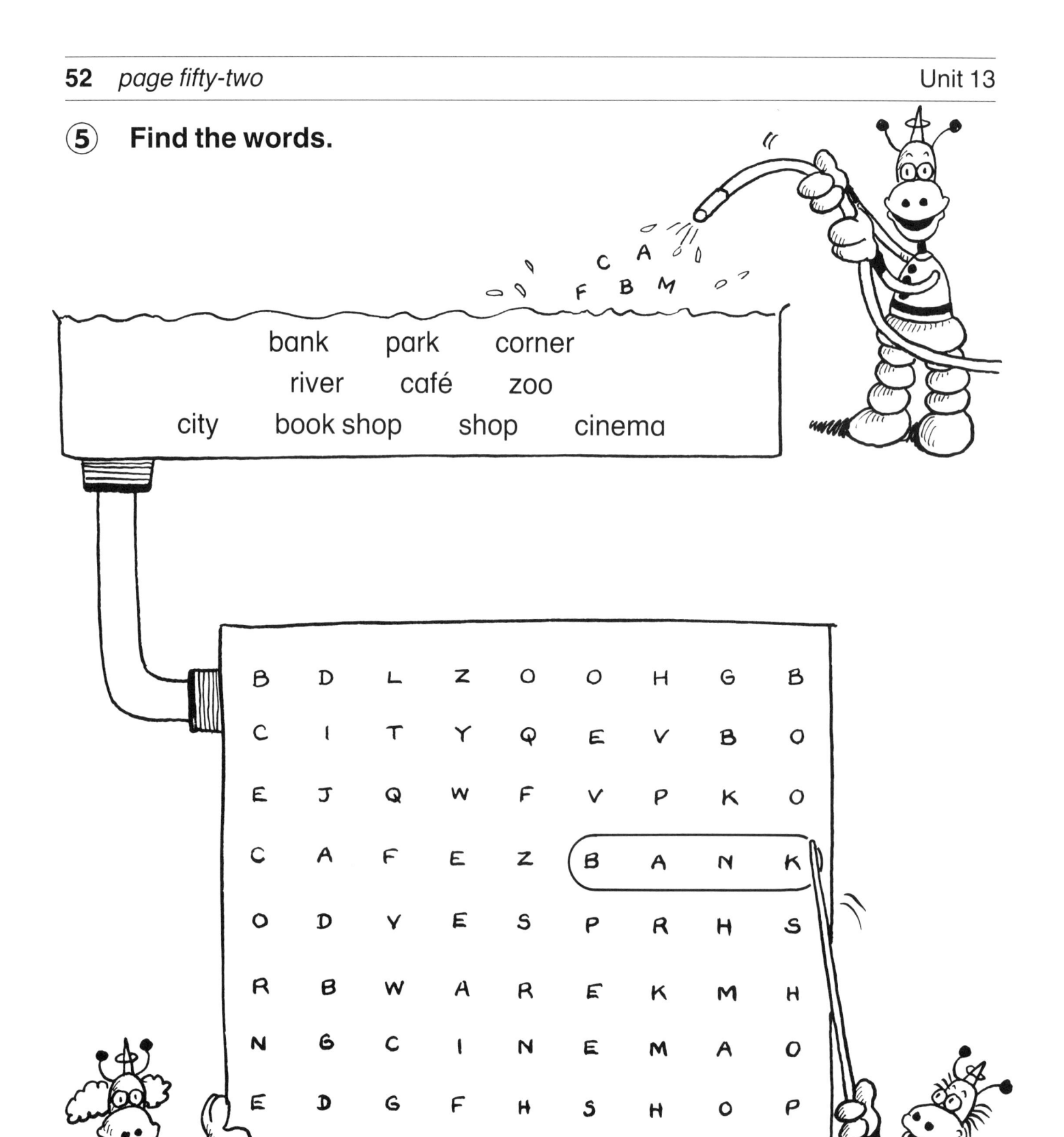

bank   park   corner
river   café   zoo
city   book shop   shop   cinema

```
B D L Z O O H G B
C I T Y Q E V B O
E J Q W F V P K O
C A F E Z B A N K
O D V E S P R H S
R B W A R E K M H
N G C I N E M A O
E D G F H S H O P
R I V E R J B L D
```

# Unit 14

*page fifty-three* **53**

**1** **What time is it? Write the answers.**

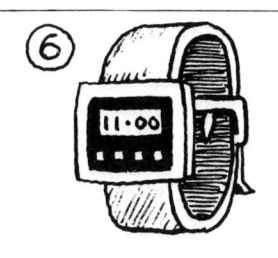

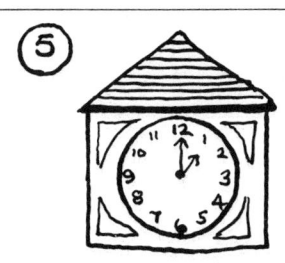

1. It's seven o'clock.

## 2 Complete the sentences.

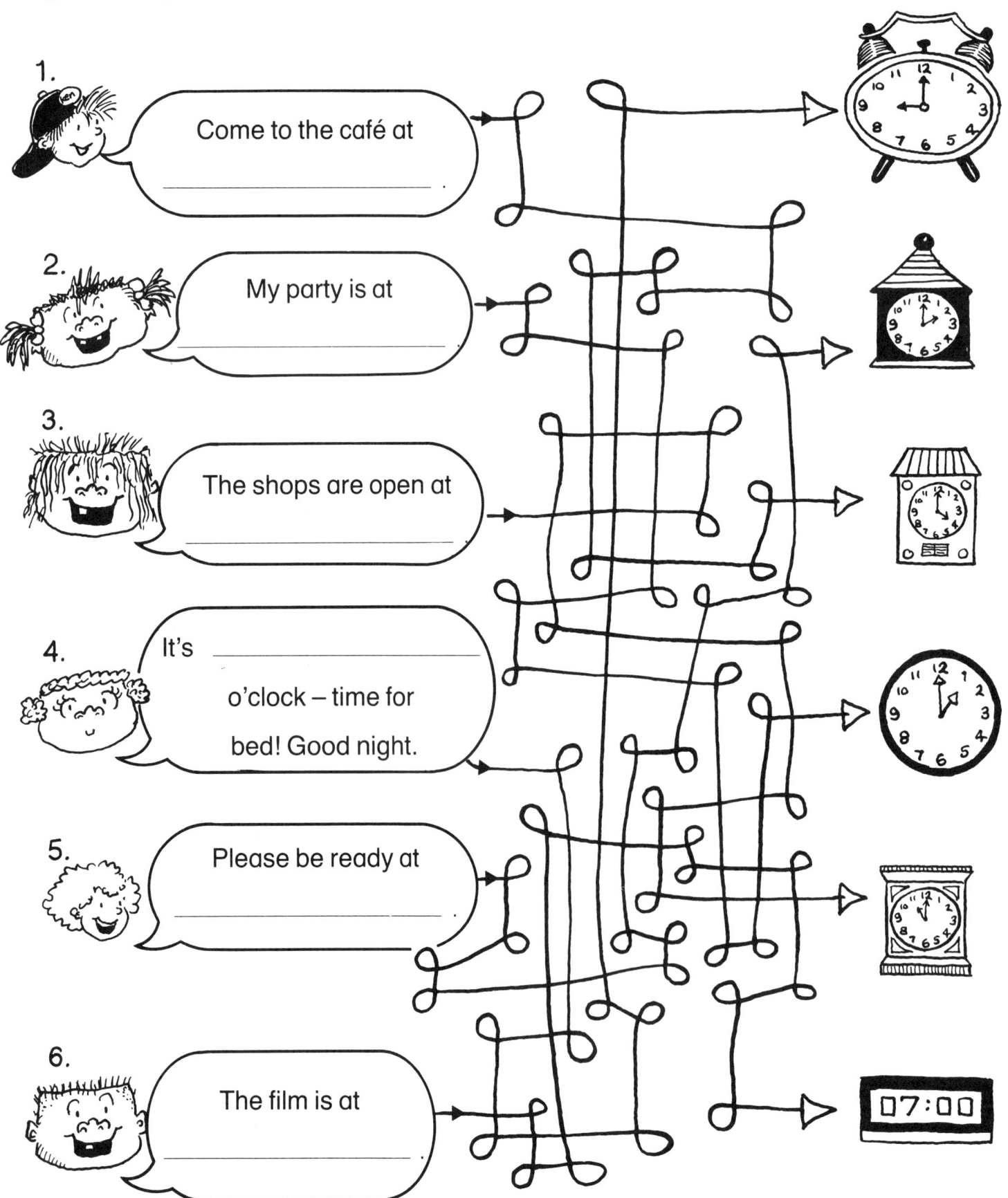

1. Come to the café at _____.

2. My party is at _____.

3. The shops are open at _____.

4. It's _____ o'clock – time for bed! Good night.

5. Please be ready at _____.

6. The film is at _____.

Unit 14                                page fifty-five

**3**     **Listen to your teacher.**

       **Listen to the *o* sound in the words.**

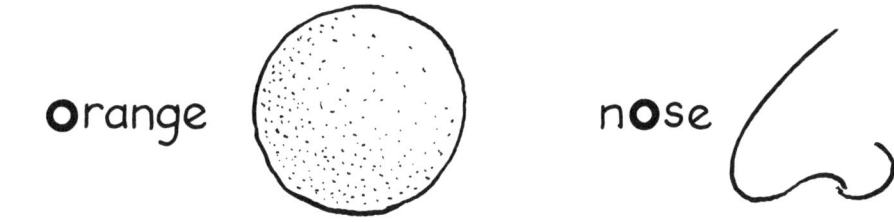

**orange**            **nose**

**Repeat the words.**

**Now say these words.**

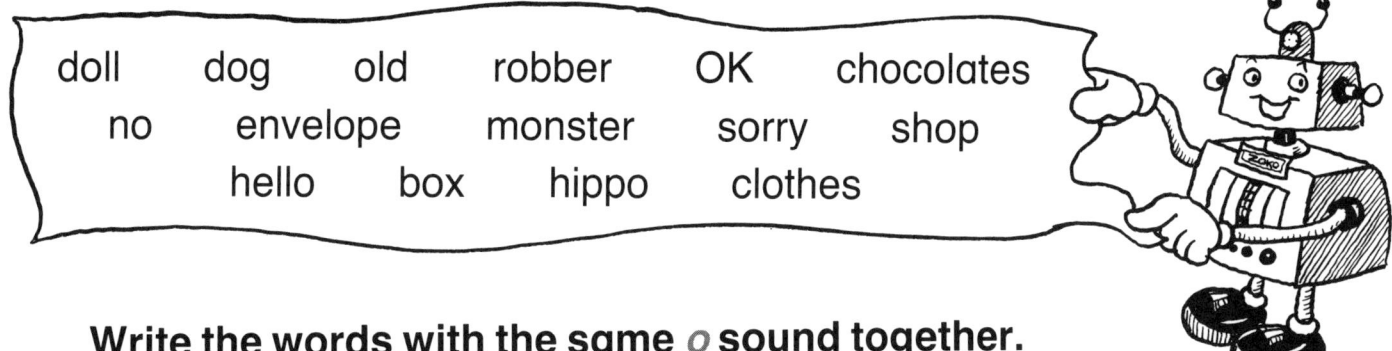

| doll | dog | old | robber | OK | chocolates |
|---|---|---|---|---|---|
| no | envelope | monster | sorry | shop | |
| hello | box | hippo | clothes | | |

**Write the words with the same *o* sound together.**

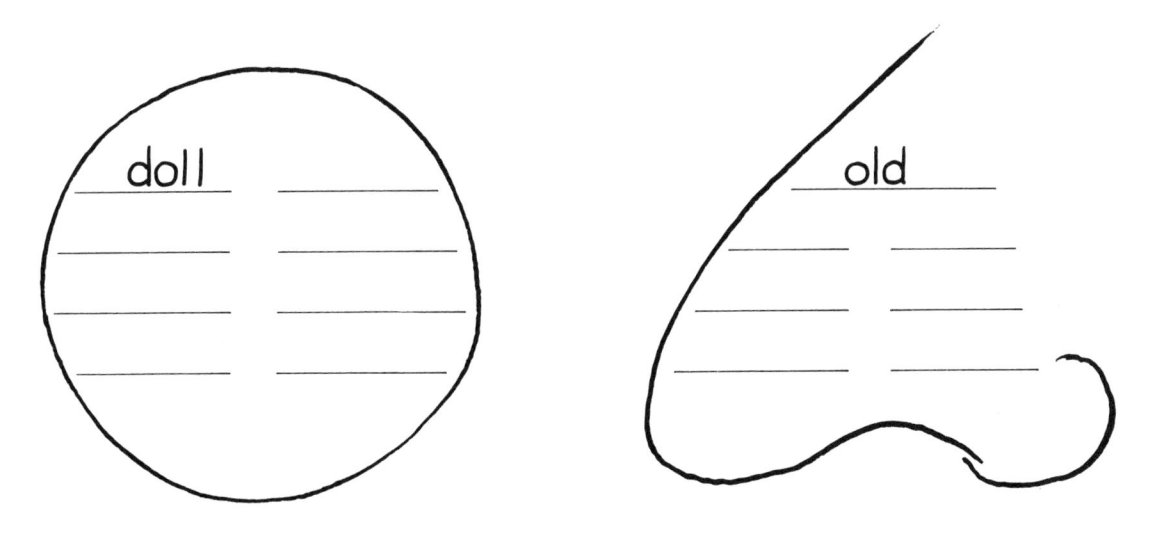

doll _____

_____ _____

_____ _____

old _____

_____ _____

_____ _____

**4**     **Find the city words.**

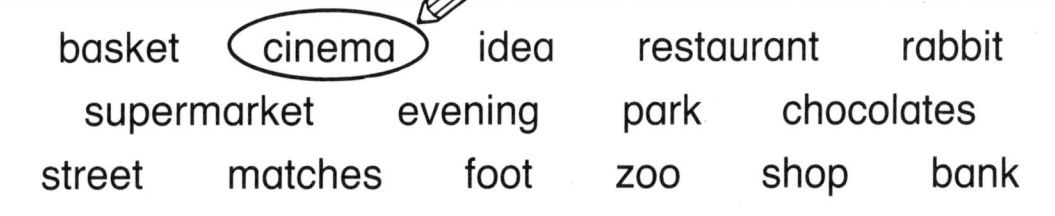

| basket | (cinema) | idea | restaurant | rabbit |
|---|---|---|---|---|
| supermarket | evening | park | chocolates | |
| street | matches | foot | zoo | shop | bank |

## 5  Read.

**METRO CINEMA**
**ROBIN HOOD**
TELEPHONE  946 726
FILM TIME  6·00

**Rex Cinema**
**Song time**
WITH MICHAEL CLACTON AND THE BLUEBIRD SISTERS
FILM TIMES  2·00 AND 7·00
TELEPHONE  878 4931

**☆ THE STAR CINEMA ☆**
**The Good Robbers**
A FILM FOR GIRLS AND BOYS
FILM TIMES  1·00, 3·00 AND 5·00
TELEPHONE  943 2262

**Now answer: right (✓) or wrong (✗)?**

1. You can see *Robin Hood* at the Metro Cinema. ..................... ✓

2. You can see the film at the Rex Cinema at two o'clock. ................. ✓

3. You can see *The Good Robbers* at seven o'clock. .................... ✓

4. There are songs in the film at the Rex Cinema. ....................... ✓

5. The telephone number of the Metro Cinema is 940 5726. ................. ✓

# Unit 15

*page fifty-seven* 57

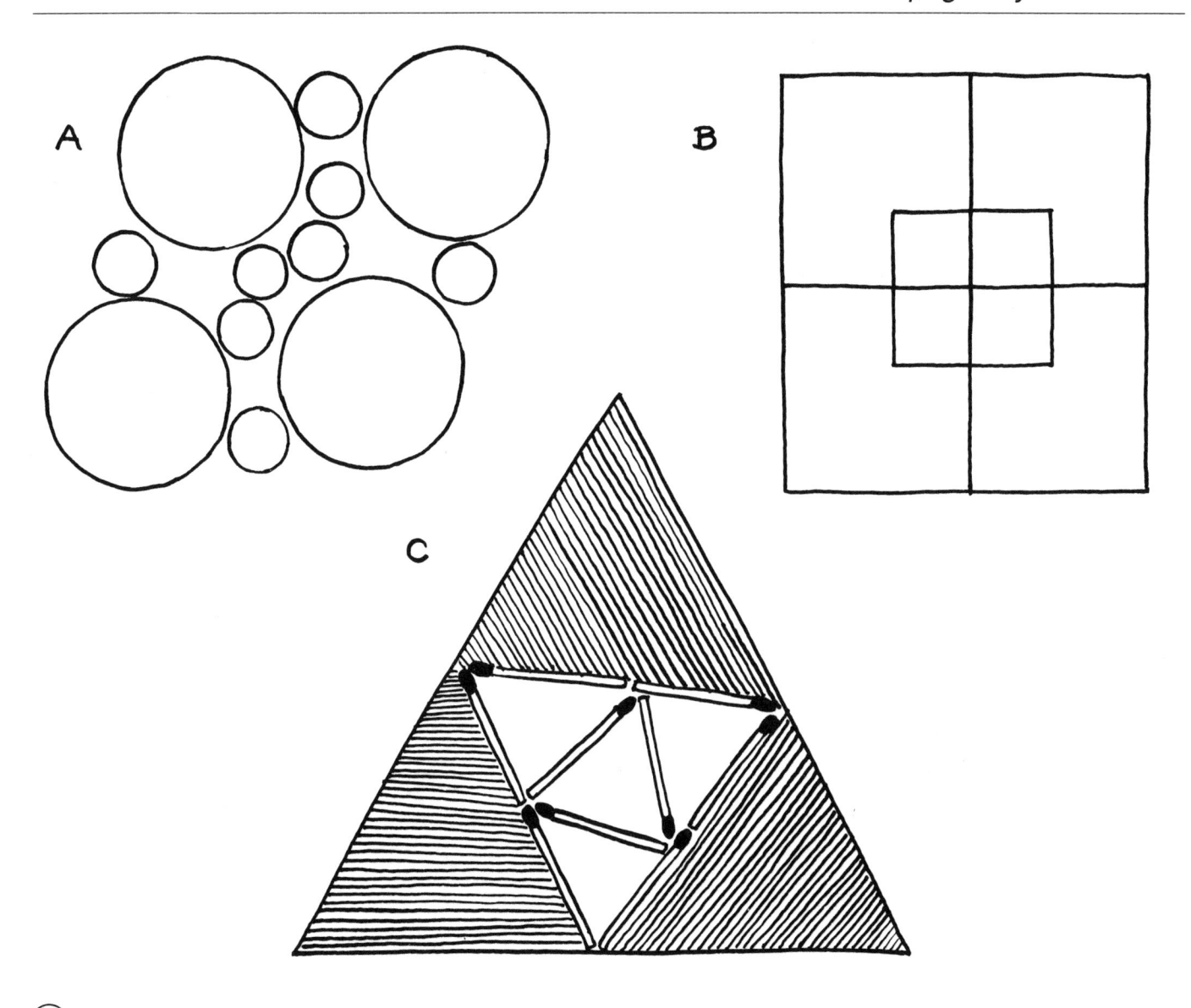

① **Answer: right (✓) or wrong (✗)?**

1. There are twelve circles in Picture A. ............... ✓ ✗
2. There are nine squares in Picture B. ............... ✓ ✗
3. There are four black triangles in Picture C. ............... ✓ ✗
4. There's one big triangle in Picture C. ............... ✓ ✗
5. There are ten triangles in Picture C. ............... ✓ ✗
6. There are ten matches in Picture C. ............... ✓ ✗

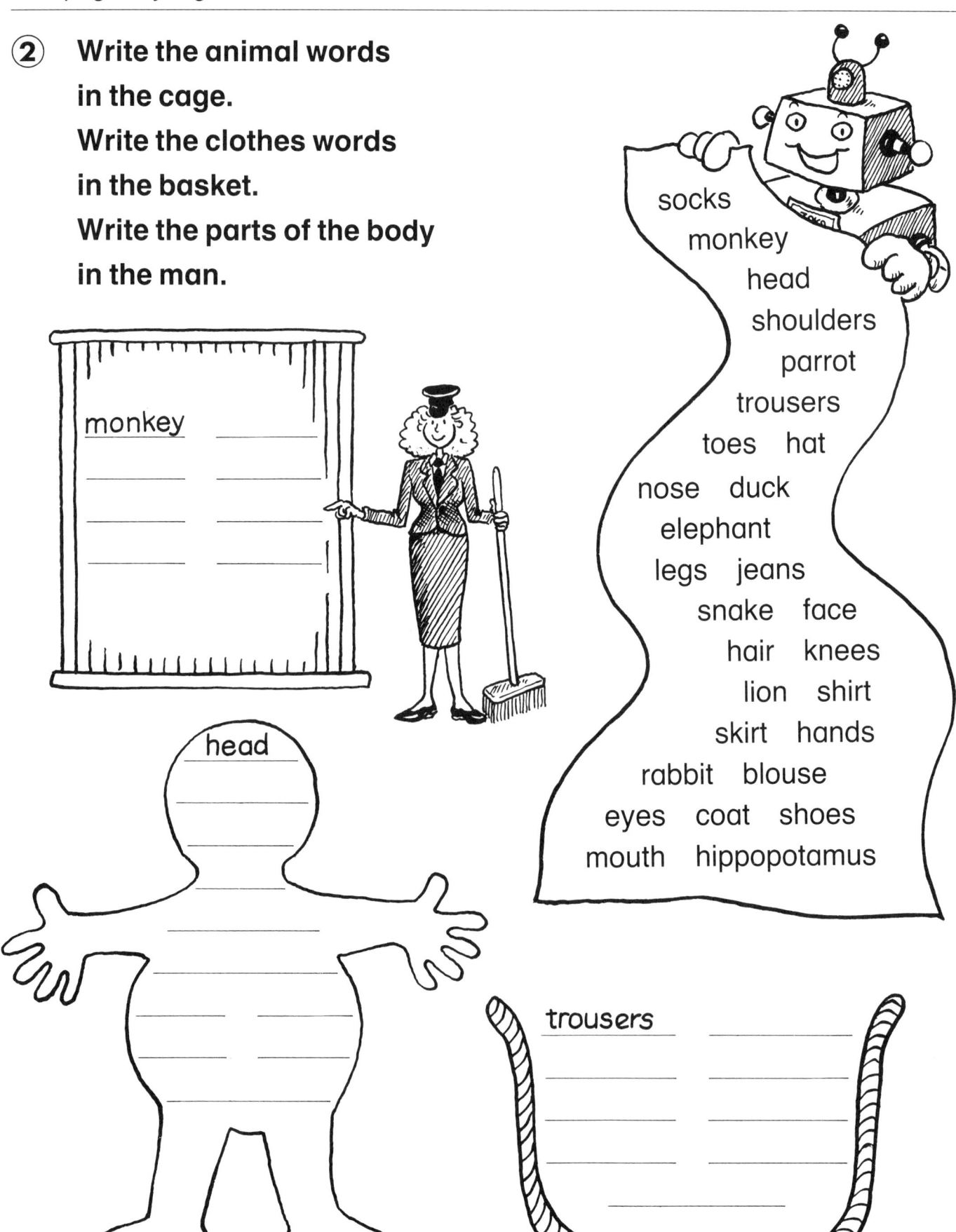

**2** **Write the animal words in the cage.**
**Write the clothes words in the basket.**
**Write the parts of the body in the man.**

socks
monkey
head
shoulders
parrot
trousers
toes   hat
nose   duck
elephant
legs   jeans
snake   face
hair   knees
lion   shirt
skirt   hands
rabbit   blouse
eyes   coat   shoes
mouth   hippopotamus

monkey

head

trousers

Unit 15                                                                page fifty-nine  59

**③  Listen to your teacher.**

**Listen to the *u* sound in the words.**

umbrella            ruler

**Repeat the words.**

**Now say these words.**

rubber    number    hungry    duck
blue    uncle    up
supermarket    Mum

**Write the words with the same *u* sound together.**

blue

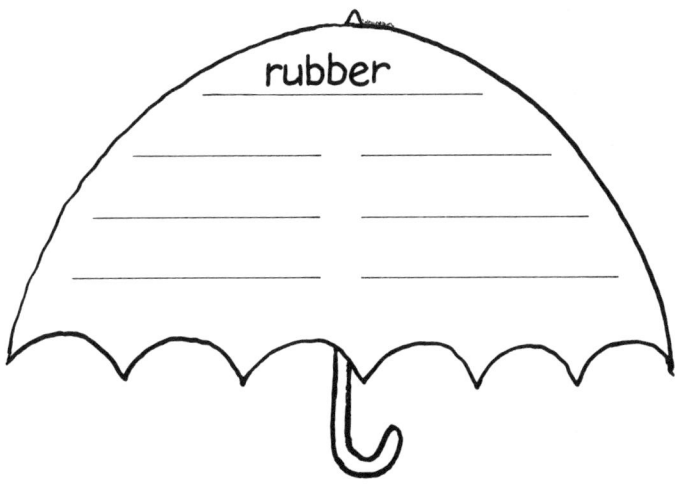

rubber

**④  Write the answers.**

1. What's your name? _____

2. How old are you? _____

3. Are you tall or short? _____

4. What colour is your hair? _____

5. What colour are your eyes? _____

# Unit 15

## ⑤ Complete the crossword.

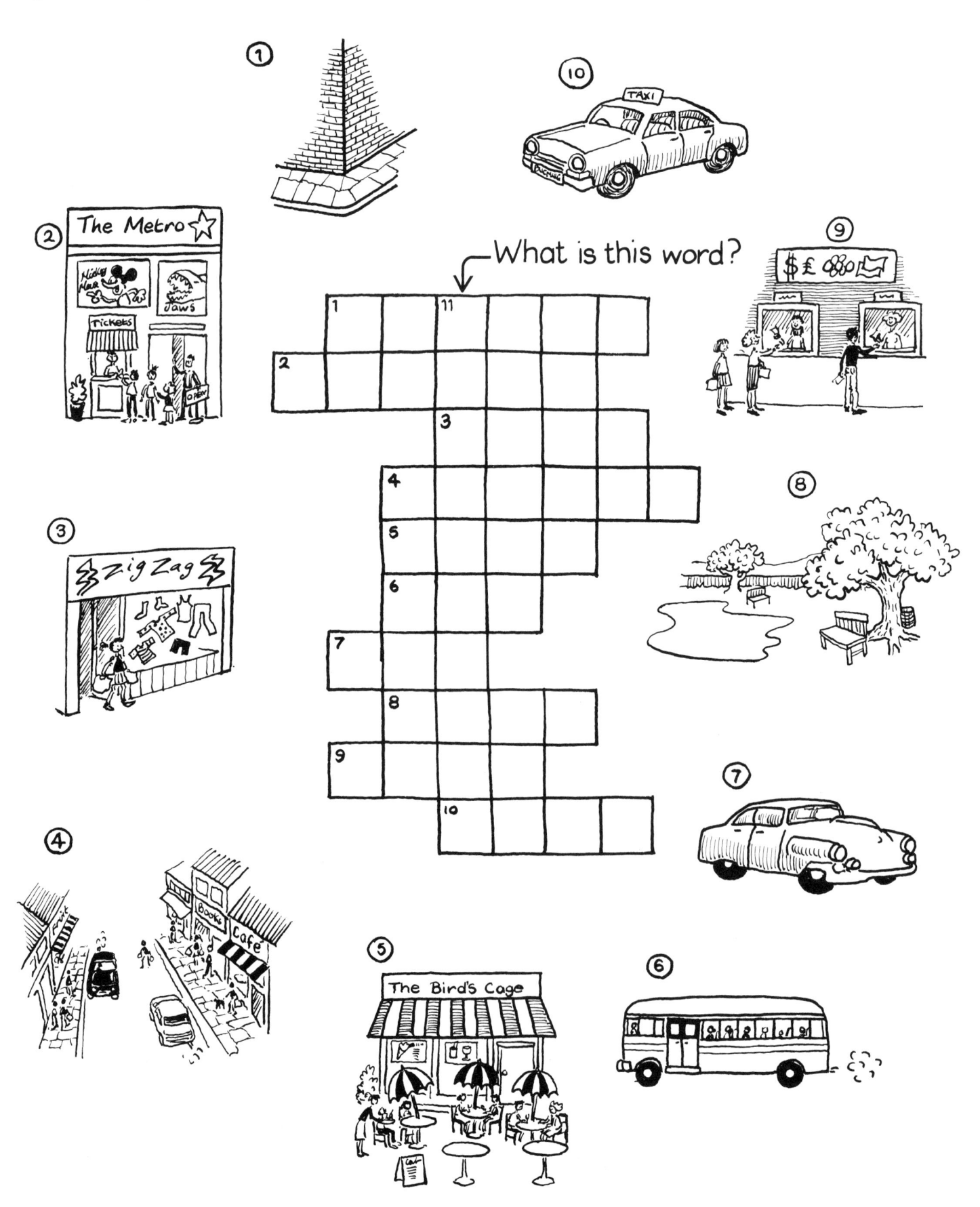

What is this word?

# Picture dictionary

page sixty-one  **61**

Complete the words.  Then colour the pictures.

b _ _ _    d _ _    e _ _ _ _ _ _ _    g _ _ _ _ _ _

h _ _ _ _    l _ _ _    m _ _ _ _ _    s _ _ _ _

z _ _    r _ _ _ _ _ _ _ _ _    b _ _ _    c _ _ _ _ _

c _ _ _    s _ _ _ _ _ _ _ _ _ _    b _ _ _  _ _ _ _    p _ _ _

**62** page sixty-two    Picture dictionary

**Complete the words.   Then colour the pictures.**

c _ _ _ _ _ _
s _ _ _

s _ _ _ _

s _ _ _ _

j _ _ _ _

t _ _ _ _ _ _ _

s _ _ _ _

b _ _ _ _ _

s _ _ _ _

c _ _ _

h _ _

t _ _ _

s _ _ _ _

y _ _ _ _

o _ _

s _ _

h _ _ _ _